Student Activity Workbook Business and Career Exploration Program

Steven T. Robinson

authorHOUSE®

AuthorHouse™
1663 Liberty Drive
Bloomington, IN 47403
www.authorhouse.com
Phone: 1-800-839-8640

First published by AuthorHouse 10/6/2011

ISBN: 978-1-4670-2468-6 (sc)
ISBN: 978-1-4670-2467-9 (e)

Library of Congress Control Number: 2011916460

Printed in the United States of America

*Any people depicted in stock imagery provided by Thinkstock are models,
and such images are being used for illustrative purposes only.
Certain stock imagery © Thinkstock.*

This book is printed on acid-free paper.

ABOUT THE BUSINESS AND CAREER EXPORATION PROGRAM STUDENT ACTIVITY WORKBOOK

If it is true that our children are most impressionable at an early age, then it's quite elementary to start providing opportunities of life changing alternatives that will help our children realize and develop toward their full potential as productive members of our society. The activities designed in this Student Activities Workbook are to be use in accordance with the Business and Career Exploration Program Curriculum.

The Business and Career Exploration Program represents a state of the art initiative and first of its kind that comprehensively provides elementary and middle school aged children with reality based positive life experiences of business and career options through personalized assembly presentations, learning projects, entrepreneurship opportunities, mentoring, visitations, and special corporate incentives. The program for many of our youngest citizens reignites the flame and dreams of what our children's lives can become.

With each educational and life experience our children gain a greater understanding of various professions and what they would like to become as working adults. The activities in this workbook are not only enjoyable, but highly interactive and challenging to promote the awareness of our children's potential.

Specific objectives of the workbook include the concept of self-knowledge, the development of a basic understanding of interests, likes and dislikes and how to interact with others, an Educational and Occupational Exploration component and a special involvement project entitled Minding My Own Business / Career Planning which facilitates the awareness of children's abilities regarding entrepreneurship opportunities.

The various activities are also designed to raise awareness of the relationship between work and learning to the needs and functions of society and the interrelationships of life roles. The elementary grades are also a good time to introduce the importance of personal responsibility and good work habits and the benefits of educational achievement.

Special Appreciation is extended to the Labor Market and Career Information Department of the Texas Workforce Commission in the collaboration of this educational publication, the US Department of Education and Ms. Molly Juliette Silbernagel for her insightful dedication in creatively designing all of the professional and or occupational artwork included in this publication.

Table of Contents

Introduction

The elementary years of a child's life are not only impressionable, but represent the most critical stages to introduce the exploration of business and career mentoring opportunities. This student activity workbook based on the Business and Career Exploration Program Curriculum, is designed to help our children through Self-Knowledge, Educational and Occupational Exploration, and the Minding My Own Business/ Career Planning Project component to think outside the box in terms of what their lives can become, while having a profound effect on how they will perceive themselves as professional working adults. The book also provides sixteen job clusters which are various types of employed positions that share common characteristics. By looking at clusters of jobs, a student may find a variety of careers with similar characteristics they may be interested in, and ultimately facilitating their desire for that particular profession.

Agriculture, Food & Natural Resources

Sample Careers
1. Pest Controller
2. Farm Equipment Mechanic
3. Veterinarian
4. Grounds Keeper
5. _____
Can you think of another?

Careers in the Agriculture, Food & Natural Resources cluster helps us to wisely utilize what Mother Natural gave us. People in these kinds of occupations can work with plants, trees and animals. They work on farms, in veterinary offices, forests or even out at sea. They mow lawns, catch fish, grow food and raise animals. You can be an engineer, pest control worker, farmer, tree pruner or forest worker and be in this cluster.

1

Business& Career Exploration Program
Pledge of Excellence

I pledge, as a child born for greatness and to do all <u>things</u>,
to allow the world to see the unlimited potential that I <u>bring</u>.

I pledge to stand in the pursuit of my goals no matter how <u>far</u>,
And if I fail to touch the sky, I know in my soul I will be hanging from a <u>star.</u>

I pledge not to fall into the traps of temptation, ignorance and <u>greed</u>.
But to learn all I can and open the doors of success using my brain as the <u>key</u>.

I pledge not to allow anyone to turn me around with their destructive <u>calls</u>,
Even if it means in order to reach my goals I have to run, walk, or <u>crawl.</u>

I pledge all that I am toward becoming a facilitator of <u>progress</u> —
marching to the sounds of my own heart and never losing <u>focus</u>.

I pledge to always to reach back and help others who remain in the shadows of <u>silence.</u> For as
I travel, we travel knowing the true meaning of community and <u>excellence</u>.

Written by,
*© **Steven T. Robinson***

Business& Career Exploration Program
Pledge of Excellence
Test 1

I pledge, as a child born for _____ and to do all_____.
to allow the world to see the unlimited _____ that I_____.

I pledge to stand in the pursuit of my _____ no matter how_____,
And if I fail to touch the _____, I know in my soul I will be hanging from a_____.

I pledge not to fall into the traps of temptation, ignorance and_____.
But to learn all I can and open the doors of success using my brain as the_____.

I pledge not to allow _____ to turn me around with their destructive_____,
Even if it means in order to reach my_____ I have to run, walk, or_____.

I pledge all that I am toward becoming a facilitator of_____ –
marching to the sounds of my own _____ and never losing_____.

I pledge to always to reach back and_____ others who remain in the shadows
of_____. For as I travel, we travel knowing the true meaning of
_____ and_____.

Business& Career Exploration Program
Pledge of Excellence
Test 2

Arts, A/V Technology & Communications

Sample Careers
1. Radio Announcer
2. Photographer
3. Jeweler
4. Writer
5. _____

Can you think of another?

Career in the Arts, Audio/Visual Technology & Communications cluster usually utilize a person's creativity. People in these occupations can work with cameras, musical instruments or small tools. They may work in TV studios, jewelry stores and theaters or be self –employed. You can be an illustrator, writer, radio announcer, reporter or film editor and be in this career cluster.

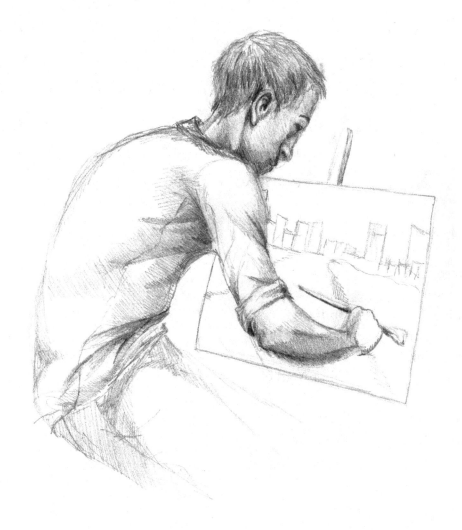

Career Search

```
R C I C U I N F O R M A T I O N N I
P E O P L Y D O E M P L O Y M E N T
R S T L S R R A J O B R I O L L R E
O F S R A P W A G E T N E S M S E T
F U A I S B B E M P L O Y O L Y L F
E N L N A E O U B T T O S I W T A A
S I A D L M M R S O T P K R I E B B
S F R U A P E U M I A S I G N M O I
I O A S R L N X N A N S L O D P R L
O N E T Y O N W P I R E L A U L M R
N N D R J Y S R O L F K S L S O A O
U I I Y L M O S A R O O E S T Y R N
K F I N T E R E S T K R R T R E S O
I A A P B O O M Y R K A E M T R N J
```

Word List

Interest	Salary
Profession	Skill
Training	Uniform
Employment	Industry
Occupation	Work
Explore	Labor Market
Job	Career
Wage	Goal
Information	Business

Business, Management & Administration

Sample Careers
1. Mail Clerk
2. Receptionist
3. Accountant
4. Human Resources Administrator
5. _____

Can you think of another?

Careers in the Business, Management & Administration cluster help to run businesses smoothly. People in these occupations can work with math, grammar, money, people and computers. They work to connect business people and provide services that help make business successful. They may work in banks, insurance offices or just about ANY business you can think of. You can be a bookkeeper, stock clerk, purchasing agent or manger and be in this cluster.

Activity: Career Name Tags

Career Name Tags – Get to Know You Activity

All activities designed in this Student Activities Workbook are to be use in accordance with the Business and Career Exploration Program Curriculum.

From information present during the activity which careers sounded most interesting and why?

_____

_____

_____

_____

_____

_____

How are these particular careers related to your own interest, abilities, aptitudes and or talents?

_____

_____

_____

_____

_____

_____

_____

The most important thing you have learned about yourself from this activity?

_____

_____

_____

_____

_____

_____

_____

Architecture & Construction

Sample Careers

1. Roofer
2. Electrician
3. Plumber
4. Architect
5. _____

Can you think of another?

Careers in the Architecture & Construction design and build things. People in these occupations can work with many different tools to help them do their special jobs. They may build or design houses and buildings out of wood, steel or stone. They build highways and bridges too. You can be an engineer, electrician, carpenter or drafter and be in this career cluster.

_____
Your Name

_____
Address

City   State   Zip Code

Objective:
(Position) _____
Experience

_____
(List the jobs you had or currently have. For example, walking the dog, babysitter or chores at home).

<u>**Job 1.**</u> _____

_____

<u>**Job 2.**</u> _____

_____

<u>**Job 3.**</u> _____

Education: _____
Grade Name of School

Special Awards or Achievements: (List awards you have received and when. For example, Honor Roll, Perfect Attendance, or any Recognition Awards).

_____
_____
_____

Abilities and Skills: (List positive character traits and things you are good at. For example, good listener, reliable, computer skills, good in math, great speller).

_____
_____
_____

References: (List people who will say good things about you).

_____
_____
_____

Education & Training

Sample Careers

1. School Teacher
2. School Principal
3. Coach
4. Librarian
5. _____

Can you think of another?

Careers in the Education & Training cluster help people learn new knowledge and get new skills. People in these occupations may work in libraries, schools or recreation centers. They may help plan or manage activities in a learning environment. You can be a teacher, counselor, librarian or a coach and be in this cluster.

Activity: Who Likes What I Like

<u>Who Likes What I Like?</u>

All activities designed in this Student Activities Workbook are to be use in accordance with the Business and Career Exploration Program Curriculum.

From information presented during the activity, what could you do now to build on your interest in ways that might lead to a career or job someday?

_____
_____
_____
_____
_____
_____
_____

What can you do to be **sure** you make the most of things you really like to do and the things you are good at doing?

_____
_____
_____
_____
_____
_____
_____

Based on this activity what is it that you would like to be when you grow up?

_____
_____
_____
_____
_____
_____
_____

Finance

Sample Careers
1. Credit Analyst
2. Accountant
3. Bank Teller
4. Insurance Adjuster
5. _____

Can you think of another?

Careers in the Finance cluster work with money. They help people and businesses account for money they spend or invest. People in these occupations use lots of math when they work. They may work in banks, insurance and tax offices or in most any business. You can be a budget analyst, cashier, insurance agent or loan officer and be in this career cluster.

Bank of America

Activity: What my life will be like?

All activities designed in this Student Activities Workbook are to be use in accordance with the Business and Career Exploration Program Curriculum.

Growing up, getting an education, maintaining a career and possibly having a family is an experience all adults have in common. In thinking about your own life as an adult, what do you think your future will be like?

What place in the world will you call home? Will you live in the city, the country or maybe the suburbs? Will you have any pets and if is so what kind, Will you get married, have children?

Write a story about your life in the future, perhaps 15 or 20 years from now. Talk about the things that will have changed, are you a different person and what responsibilities you will have.

_____

_____

_____

_____

_____

_____

_____

_____

_____

_____

_____

_____

_____

_____

_____

_____

_____

Health Science

Careers in the Health Science cluster help people stay healthy or take care of people who are sick. People in these occupations might specialize on different parts of your body like your teeth, feet, eyes, back or even your brain. They may work in hospitals, laboratories, pharmacies, dentist offices or schools. You can be a psychiatrist, optician, pharmacist, nurse or chiropractor and be in this cluster.

Activity: Career Replay

<u>Career Reply</u>

All activities designed in this Student Activities Workbook are to be use in accordance with the Business and Career Exploration Program Curriculum.

Divide students into three equal relay teams of 2 to 10 players each. Tell students they are going to play a relay game where they try to think of as many community jobs or careers as possible in three minutes (or an amount of time you designate).
When the leader (you) calls out "Start," the first player on each team goes to the title area, picks up a marker, writes down a community career and takes the marker to the next player in line. Then, the first player goes to the end of the line. Play continues with each player taking as many turns as possible during the three-minute time period and the leader calls "Stop."

For Activity Follow Up - Relevance and Discussion
Please review lesson plan covered in the Curriculum Manuel.

Training helps people connect with job opportunities. List your school / work responsibilities that can help you prepare for a job in the future?

1._____

2._____

3._____

4._____

5._____

6._____

7._____

8._____

9._____

10._____

Hospitality & Tourism

Sample Careers
1. Hotel Manager
2. Chef
3. Amusement Park Operator
4. Recreation Worker
5. _____

Can you think of another?

Careers in the Hospitality & Tourism cluster help people have a safe and good time when they are traveling or visiting new places. People in these occupations can work with food, sports or amusement parks rides. They may work in restaurants, hotels or amusement parks. You can be a banker, flight attendant, travel agent or hotel manager and be in this cluster.

Activity: Guest Speaker

Guest Speaker – Questions & Answers

All activities designed in this Student Activities Workbook are to be use in accordance with the Business and Career Exploration Program Curriculum.

Selected Profession: _____

Questions I would like to ask:

_____

_____

_____

_____

Answers Provided:

_____

_____

_____

_____

What did I learn about this person and their career?

_____

_____

_____

_____

How important is staying in school and getting a good education to getting a good job or career as an adult?

_____

_____

_____

_____

Based on what you would like to be when you grow up, how has this career presentation helped you?

_____

_____

_____

_____

Human Services

Sample Careers
1. Funeral Director
2. Child Care Worker
3. Social Worker
4. Residential Counselor
5. _____

Can you think of another?

Career in the Human cluster prepare people to help families and communities. People in these occupations work closely with others, examples include helping people with childcare, family counseling or investigations. They may work in funeral homes, preschools or counseling offices. You can be a minister, counselor, nursing aide or therapist and be in this cluster.

Activity: B.C.E.P Interview

<u>The Interview</u>

All activities designed in this Student Activities Workbook are to be use in accordance with the Business and Career Exploration Program Curriculum.

Interview a person who works in a career in which you are interested. Some questions you might want to ask are:

1. Where is your job located?

2. What is your position and responsibilities at work?

3. How did you choose the career that was best for you?

4. Did you always know what you wanted to be when you were young?

5. What part of your education is important to your job and why?

6. In school or on your job, did you ever make a mistake and what did you learn?

7. What is the most difficult part of your job?

8. Did you go to college or require any special training for your career or job?

9. What gives you the most satisfaction about your job?

10. What subjects in school did you take that are used throughout your day?

11. What type of student were you in school?

12. Based on your accomplishments what words of encouragement would you give?

13. How many and what careers did you think about before picking the one you have now?

14. Did you ever feel like it was impossible to be what you are now, and what made it change?

15. Do you have any children; if so how old are they and what are their names?

16. How do you relax or have fun when you're not working?

17. What is the difference between having a money making career and having a career that makes you happy?

Information Technology

Sample Careers
1. Help Desk Technician
2. Webmaster
3. Cable TV Installer
4. Computer Programmer
5. _____

Can you think of another?

Careers in the Information Technology cluster are usually very technical. People in these occupations usually work with computers and lots of information. They may work in almost any business where computers are used. They may develop computers programs and hardware. You can be a Web master, programmer or database or administrator and be in this career cluster.

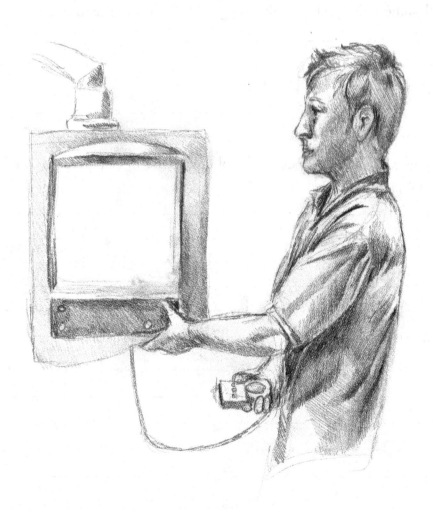

Activity: Let's Talk a Minute

Let's Talk a Minute

All activities designed in this Student Activities Workbook are to be use in accordance with the Business and Career Exploration Program Curriculum.

Based on what you have learned from other students and about yourself during this activity,

1. What do you need to learn now to get ready for a good job when you grow up?

_____

_____

_____

_____

_____

2. How will doing well in school help you get a good job in the future?

_____

_____

_____

_____

_____

3. What things can you do outside of school now that will help prepare you for getting a a good job as an adult?

_____

_____

_____

_____

_____

4. What can you do with free time that will help you be a successful person?

_____

_____

_____

_____

_____

Law, Public Safety & Security

Sample Careers
1. Lawyer
2. Security Officer
3. Firefighter
4. Police Officer
5. _____
Can you think of another?

Careers in the Law, Public Safety & Security cluster help protect the people living in he community. They may work in law offices, police stations, fire stations or jails. You can be a sheriff, judge, emergency medical technician (EMT) or warden and be in this cluster.

JUDGE SMITH

Activity: Communication Blocks

Communication Blocks

All activities designed in this Student Activities Workbook are to be use in accordance with the Business and Career Exploration Program Curriculum.

Directions: Begin by saying that working together requires good communication. This is true at home, at school, in the community, and in the world of work. In this game, students face a communication challenge. Here is the challenge: The two players sit back to back. In front of each player are up to ten blocks or objects, each with the exact same shapes and sizes as the other player has. Have one player quickly build a small structure using the objects in front of their team. Without turning around, the player attempts to give verbal instructions to the other player so that the other player can build an identical structure with his/her blocks. The other player may ask questions to clarify the instructions whenever he/she needs more information or help.

For Activity Follow Up - Relevance and Discussion
Please review lesson plan covered in the Curriculum Manuel.

Student Summary:
From participating in this activity, the most important thing I learned was,

_____

_____

_____

_____

_____

_____

_____

_____

_____

_____

_____

_____

_____

_____

Transportation, Distribution & Logistics

Sample Careers
1. Ship Captain
2. Automotive Mechanic
3. School Bus Driver
4. Airplane Pilot
5. _____

Can you think of another?

Careers in the Transportation, Distribution & Logistics cluster move people, material and goods safely. People in these occupations can work with cars, busses, trucks, trains, boats and airplanes. They may work in the air, on the ocean or on highways moving things from one place to another. You can be a taxi driver, engineer, air traffic controller or mechanic and be in this career cluster.

Mystery Code

Write the answer to each word puzzle in the spaces below. When all the blanks have been filled in, use the circled letters to complete the mystery code at the bottom of the page.

1. Employed positions require us all to get an ⭕⭕⭕⭕⭕⭕⭕⭕⭕.

2. It takes a lot of __ __ __ ⭕ __ __ __ __ to be involved in ⭕ __ __ __ __ __ __ careers.

3. People who work just for the experience and without pay are called __ __ __ __ __ ⭕ __ __ __

4. In order to make an educated decision we must have good __ __ __ ⭕ __ __ __ __ __ __.

5. The more education we have increases the __ __ __ __ __ __ ⭕ we have in life.

6. __ __ __ __ __ ⭕ __ __ __ __, cell phones and the Internet are examples of modern __ __ ⭕ __ __ __ __ __ __.

7. Careers that consist of money management and recorded keeping help us with our daily __ __ __ __ __ ⭕⭕

8. Good luck in completing the __ __ ⭕⭕ __ __ __ below.

Use this list to find the correct words to fit in the blanks.

FINANCE   INFORMATION   SCIENCE   COMPUTERS
VOLUNTEERS   CHOICES   MESSAGE
TECHNOLOGY   TRAINING   EDUCATION

Mystery Code

__ __ __ __ __ __ __ __ __ - __ __ the key __ __ - __ __ __ __ __ __ __ __.

26

Manufacturing

Sample Careers
1. Chemical Equipment Operator
2. Machinist
3. Welder
4. Electronic Assembler
5. _____
Can you think of another?

Career in the Manufacturing cluster involve turning raw materials into final consumer products. People in these occupations can work with big machines, precision tools and computers to assemble parts or build products. They may work in large buildings, outside or in warehouses. You can be many types of engineer, machine operator, electrician or quality control technician and be in this cluster.

Activity: Set Your Own Money Goals

<u>Set Your Own Money Goals</u>

All activities designed in this Student Activities Workbook are to be use in accordance with the Business and Career Exploration Program Curriculum.

For Activity Follow Up - Relevance and Discussion
Please review lesson plan covered in the Curriculum Manuel.

Realistic Money Goals

<u>Short –Term Money Goals</u>

_____
_____
_____
_____
_____
_____

<u>Long –Term Money Goals</u>

_____
_____
_____
_____
_____
_____

<u>Student Questionnaire</u>: **(Yes or No)**

Do you have with parental involvement a Saving Account at a bank? _____

Are you making money doing chores at home for family or friends? _____

Would you like to become an entrepreneur or have your own business? _____

Instead of spending money, are you trying to save as much as possible? _____

Class discussion - what are some ways kids can make money?

Government & Public Administration

Sample Careers
1. Highway Maintenance Worker
2. Postal Mail Carrier
3. Water Treatment Operator
4. City Manager
5. _____

Can you think of another?

Careers in the Government & Public Administration cluster work in our local and federal government. They help people get government services such as driver's licenses and building permits. They enforce regulations so that roads and bridges are built safety and air and water remain clean. People in these occupations work with the public and are sometimes elected into their jobs. They may work in offices or even outdoors. You can be an elected official, like the President or mayor, or be a tax collector, highway maintenance worker or mail carrier and be in this career cluster.

Name Decoder

Decode the list of names in order to find out their profession. The first one is done for you.

Tod Roc Doctor

Nu Ress _____

W.R Laye _____

Ed. Tints _____

Act E. Her _____

Ted P. Seri _____

T. Poli _____

Tes C. Sar _____

Chan C. Mei _____

Peter Carn _____

Rita C. Clein _____

Mary O. _____

Drew Le _____

Ber P. Lum _____

Eve Deitt _____

Words to choose from:

Welder	Pilot	President	Detective	Teacher
Mechanic	Dentist	Carpenter	Lawyer	Nurse
Mayor	Electrician	Plumber	Actress	

Science, Technology, Engineering & Mathematics

Sample Careers
1. Biological Scientist
2. Chemical Engineer
3. Drafter
4. Robotics Technician
5. _____
Can you think of another?

Careers in the Science, Technology, Engineering & Mathematics cluster are usually very technical. Employed people are good at problem solving and measuring things. People in these occupations may do lots of research. They may work in laboratories or in offices. You can be an engineer, archeologist, astronomer, meteorologist and be in this cluster.

Activity: Self Portrait / Public Speaking

<u>Self Portrait / Public Speaking</u>

All activities designed in this Student Activities Workbook are to be use in accordance with the Business and Career Exploration Program Curriculum.

In this exercise dressed professionally, students will be required to write and give three short speeches over time in front of their peers. This activity not only helps students develop a Self Portrait of Confidence, but also helps them to understand how to interact with people and present themselves in various situations that maybe career or work related. Student presentations with parental consent maybe videotaped for evaluation and or critic purpose. Working with program facilitators suggested topics of interest may include,

<u>Informative Speech</u>

_____

_____

_____

_____

_____

_____

<u>Augmentative Speech</u>

_____

_____

_____

_____

_____

<u>Persuasive Speech</u>

_____

_____

_____

_____

_____

_____

Marketing, Sales & Service

Sample Careers
1. Purchasing Manager
2. Cashier
3. Real Estate Agent
4. Hairdresser
5. _____
Can you think of another?

Careers in the Marketing, Sales & Service cluster sell products or services. People in these occupations may work in an office or spend time traveling as they sell the product made by the company for which they work. They will sometimes have to do research and figure out what people want to buy or how much they would be willing to pay for a product. You can be a sales executive, store manager, advertising manager or customer service representative and be in this cluster.

Activity: Better Business – Better Community

Better Business – Better Community

All activities designed in this Student Activities Workbook are to be use in accordance with the Business and Career Exploration Program Curriculum.

For Activity Follow Up - Relevance and Discussion
Please review the purpose of Better Business – Better Community covered in the Curriculum Manuel.

How important do you think it is for businesses to contribute to making the community a better place to live?

_____

_____

_____

_____

_____

How could giving some of their profits away to the community help businesses be more successful?

_____

_____

_____

_____

_____

If you were running a business today, would you want your business to help make the community a better place? Why or why not?

_____

_____

_____

_____

_____

Write a brief story about a fantasy business that helps make the community a better place.

Minding My Own Business / Career Planning
Working with Students to Create a Business

All activities designed in this Student Activities Workbook are to be use in accordance with the Business and Career Exploration Program Curriculum.

For Activity Follow Up – Relevance, Discussion and Implementation
Please review the complete project covered in the Curriculum Manuel. Page 110

Minding My Own Business / Career Planning
Working with Students to Create a Business

All activities designed in this Student Activities Workbook are to be use in accordance with the Business and Career Exploration Program Curriculum.

For Activity Follow Up – Relevance, Discussion and Implementation
Please review the complete project covered in the Curriculum Manuel. Page 110

Purpose and Goals
Building on students' growing business knowledge and skills, this phase of the BCEP helps students learn how to start up and operate their own businesses. In collaboration with Project Facilitators, School Personnel (Teachers, Librarians, School Principal and others), Career Mentors and Role Models help students develop a plan for creating a product or service and selling it to potential customers. Project facilitators, career mentors and role models such as classroom teachers, librarians, school principals, and parents can play a vital role to the implementation of a successful business.

The Project Facilitators
The Project Facilitators takes a lead role in identifying and coordinating resources to support the project – human resources, facility resources, and material resources. Here are some of the things Project Facilitators do to ensure students have a successful business development experience:

- Talk with classroom Teachers about children's emerging business interests.

- Brainstorm ideas with Career Mentors and Role Models who are willing to participate in a Minding My Own Business project. Discuss financial and other resources that may be needed to support the start-up and implementation of the project.

- Facilitate group discussions with students to identify products and services they might like to use as the basis for a business development idea.

- Schedule and facilitate initial discussions about business development among students, Teachers, Career Mentors and Role Models.

- Inform the Librarian and School Principal about the Mind My Own Business project. Ask for help in securing resources needed (books, DVDs, access to equipment, space, the Internet, etc.). Give regular updates to the Librarian and School Principal, including "thank you" notes for support and help received.

- Gather resources from other sources that may be used to support the project (pamphlets, brochures, advertising samples, information about local business networks and organizations, etc.) Work with the classroom Teacher to develop Minding My Own Business news updates for parents. Encourage parents to get involved as the project unfolds.

Classroom Teachers

Classroom Teachers have valuable information about the readiness, abilities, skills, and career interests of students participating in BCEP. They have knowledge and understanding of students' strengths and weaknesses. They have important insights about areas where students can assume leadership and initiative and where they need help, support, and direction. They are also acutely aware of skill areas where students excel and where they face challenges.

- Share information about individual student's readiness, abilities, skills, and career interests (within the guidelines for sharing information established by the School).

- Help the Project Facilitator locate appropriate math and reading games and activities related to business development and entrepreneurship (puzzles, word searches, crosswords, sample "real world" problems involving math, board games, etc.).

- Talk with the Project Facilitator and Career Mentors or Role Models about career and business interests you have heard your students express or seen them demonstrate.

- Help the Project Facilitator and Career Mentors or Role Models identify students that could provide leadership for Minding My Own Business, exhibit good problem solving skills, exhibit imagination and creativity, or have untapped characteristics, traits, or abilities that could be nurtured and encouraged through the Minding My Own Business Project.

- Help the Project Facilitator work with the Librarian to identify resources that would be useful to the project.

Librarians

There are now many media resources available to help students learn about careers and the world of business. Here are some of the ways Librarians can help enhance the project.

- Help the Project Facilitator, classroom Teacher, and students locate books, magazines, DVDs and other media resources that are closely related to the Minding My Own Business project being developed.

- Set up a temporary special display in the library that displays resources related to the project.

- Provide assistance to students who do research related to the project during the school day.

- Create a special bulletin board display featuring resources related to the project as the project unfolds.

SCHOOL PRINCIPALS

The School Principal can provide valuable support for the Minding My Own Business project. Here are some ways that the School Principal can help the project succeed:

- Encourage other school staff to support the project and the Project Facilitator by sharing needed resources, space, equipment, materials, and expertise as needed.

- Publicize the Minding My Own Business project in school communications to Teachers and other School Personnel, communications to parents, and community news releases about school events.

- Visit the program periodically to ask students questions about their project, encourage their efforts, share ideas, and give them feedback and advice (from a consumers point of view).

- Help the project locate an appropriate venue for launching, operating, and promoting their business on the school site if appropriate.

PARENTS

- Parents have valuable insights and knowledge to share about the interests, abilities, talents, and skills their children demonstrate at home and in the community. They often know about their children's emerging hopes and dreams for the future. And, sometimes they have serious concerns about the path their children are taking. Parents who see their children becoming involved in positive projects like Minding My Own Business are likely to have renewed hope and enthusiasm about their children's prospects for the future.

If parents receive information about the project from the school and the classroom Teacher, there are a variety of ways parents can contribute to helping their children have successful experiences in the project:

- Share information about their children's special interests and talents – especially those abilities and interests that students may not readily exhibit at school.

- Talk about the project with children at home – ask questions, give feedback, share ideas.

- Help the Project Facilitator or classroom Teacher identify and gather resources, especially recyclable materials.

- Participate in "market surveys" or "opinion polls" about the marketability of the product or service the project plans to offer.

- Become a customer when the time is right!

MINDING MY OWN BUSINESS PROJECTS
Minding My Own Business projects provide Career Mentors and Role Models with an opportunity to provide leadership to students in a joint business venture. Depending on students' interests, the project may or may not be closely related to the mentor's field or career. However as students begin to create a business, the Career Mentor or Role Model uses his or her general knowledge of good business practices and entrepreneurship to help students develop their own ideas.

As students work on their business ideas, they are strongly encouraged to recognize the importance of working with others in positive, productive, and ethical ways. With this in mind, project activities promote the following behaviors:

1. To be honest and accountable to those who entrust them with their money and other valuable property;
2. To share and discuss business ideas in respectful, polite ways;
3. To solve conflicts with others through negotiation and compromise;
4. To make thoughtful business decisions about the right and/or fair thing to do;
5. To collaborate with others to achieve one's goals.

Activity: Student Project and Implementation

<u>Student Project and Implementation</u>

All activities designed in this Student Activities Workbook are to be use in accordance with the Business and Career Exploration Program Curriculum.

For Activity Follow Up – Relevance, Discussion and Implementation
Please review the complete project covered in the Curriculum Manuel. Page 123.

<u>Product or Service Development</u>

_____
_____
_____
_____
_____
_____
_____

<u>Price</u>

_____
_____
_____
_____
_____

Promotion and Publicity

_____

_____

_____

_____

_____

_____

_____

Productive Resources

_____

_____

_____

_____

_____

_____

_____

Product Placement and Delivery

_____

_____

_____

_____

_____

_____

_____

Finances/Budget

_____

_____

_____

_____

_____

_____

_____

Activity: Student Project and Implementation

Answer Key

Career Search Page 7.

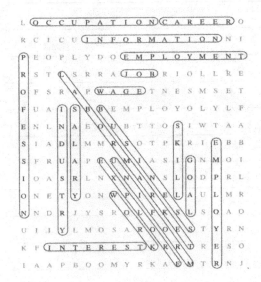

Mystery Code Page 27.

1. EDUCATION
2. TRAINING - SCIENCE
3. VOLUNTEERS
4. INFORMATION
5. CHOICES
6. COMPUTERS - TECHNOLOGY
7. FINANCE
8. MESSAGE

E D U C A T I O N - I S - the key - T O - S U C C E S S.

Answer Key

Name Decoder Page 31.

Name: Profession:
Ted Rocs Doctor
Nu Ress Nurse
W.R Laye Lawyer
Act E. Her Teacher
Ted P. Seri President
T. Poli Pilot
Tea C. Sar Actress
Chan C. Mei Mechanic
Peter Carn Carpenter
Rita C. Clein Electrician
Mary O Mayor
Drew Le Welder
Ber P. Lum Plumber
Eve Deitt Detective

Printed in the United States
By Bookmasters